IO209453

Anonymous

Indiana's gift to the battleship Indiana

Anonymous

Indiana's gift to the battleship Indiana

ISBN/EAN: 9783337306236

Printed in Europe, USA, Canada, Australia, Japan

Cover: Foto ©ninafisch / pixelio.de

More available books at **www.hansebooks.com**

STORY OF THE SUBSCRIPTION

ACCOUNT OF THE PRESENTATION

DESCRIPTION OF THE

SILVER SERVICE

LIST OF BOOKS AND NAMES OF

THE SUBSCRIBERS

Indiana

OUR Land—our Home—the common home indeed
  Of soil-born children and adopted ones—
  The stately daughters and the stalwart sons
Of Industry:—All greeting and godspeed!
O home to proudly live for, and, if need
  Be, proudly die for, with the roar of guns
  Blent with our latest prayer.—So died men once. . . .
Lo, Peace! As we look on the land they freed—
Its harvests all in ocean-overflow
  Poured round autumnal coasts in billowy gold—
    Its corn and wine and balméd fruits and flowers,—
We know the exaltation that they know
  Who now, steadfast inheritors, behold
    The Land Elysian, marveling "This is ours!"

JAMES WHITCOMB RILEY.

Indianapolis, September, 1896.

Story of the Gift

HE story of the subscription for the purpose of presenting a silver service and a library to the Battleship INDIANA is one that reflects great credit on the people of the commonwealth in whose honor the ship was named. It is seldom that subscriptions have been so entirely spontaneous, so varied in character, so thoroughly representative of a people in all the various relations of society. The first announcement of the purpose was made by *The Indianapolis News*, in 1890, immediately after the publication of the decision by the Navy Department that this ship, the first battleship of the new navy, was to be called the INDIANA. It was renewed at the time the ship was launched, in February, 1893.

The Beginning of the Subscription

The movement to secure the subscription was begun by *The Indianapolis News*, in June, 1894. In an editorial, on the 28th of that month, that paper set out the proposed scope and method in words worth reproducing, because they are now a record of what happened. Referring to its announcement, when the ship was named, that at the proper time it would undertake to raise a subscription for the purpose, it said :

"*The News* will undertake the subscription. It will collect and account for all sums committed to it in this behalf; will speak for the public feeling on the subject; will, in due time, suggest the appointment of a committee to select a design for this token. We believe we shall need only to bring the matter fully to the attention of Indianians to secure easily the sum that will be required. This must be, judging by the experience of others, not less than $8,000. There is wide limit as to cost; but there is no very wide limit, and this is fortunate, in the choice of a token. * * * We must have a handsome silver service. We should also have a suitable library. These two things can be secured for about $8,000— not less. If it should be more, all the better. But that sum at least the willing spirit of the good people of the State of Indiana should undertake to make up.

"Every town in Indiana should be represented in this. We want dollars and dimes. No gift is too large; none is too small, and there should be no town from the lake to the river, from Ohio to Illinois, that should be unaccounted for in making up this sum. *The News* will start the subscription with $100. It appeals to its esteemed contemporaries, local and general throughout the State, to be represented in the subscription. It appeals to every citizen of Indiana of whatever station in life, public or private, of whatever standard of prosperity, to be among those who shall contribute this recognition to the great battleship INDIANA."

The response was as gratifying as it was immediate. The first publication of names was made four days after the announcement. It was as follows:

Governor Claude Matthews	$100 00
Ex-Governor A. G. Porter	100 00
Attorney-General A. G. Smith	100 00
State Auditor Oscar B. Henderson	50 00
A. M. Sweeney, Clerk Supreme Court	25 00
William R. Myers, Secretary of State	25 00
Otto N. Frenzel	25 00
John P. Frenzel	25 00
John H. Holliday	50 00
Albert J. Beveridge	25 00
Sterling R. Holt	25 00
Leon Bailey	25 00
John L. Griffiths	25 00
A. F. Potts	25 00
Lew Wallace	25 00
George G. Tanner	25 00
Albert Sahm	25 00
V. T. Malott	25 00
The Indianapolis News	100 00
Total to date	$825 00

Progress of the Subscription

A few days later, the Muncie *Herald* suggested that Muncie, the "greatest gas city on earth," should make up a fund and give it in the name of the city. *The News* encouraged this friendly rivalry, and as the subscription shows the chief cities of Indiana are each represented. The New Albany *Ledger* urged a subscription in its town. The Terre Haute *Gazette* and the Madison *Courier* followed suit. The Lafayette *Courier*, the Jeffersonville *News* and other papers early advocated the cause.

Current affairs drew popular attention in other directions constantly, but the subscription grew slowly—by November, 1894, amounting to $1,050. But whether the subscription went slowly or fast no stimulus was ever applied to it, beyond the repeated appeals to the people which appeared in *The Indianapolis News* and occasionally in some of the other newspapers in the State. It was the voluntary gift of the people.

The state of the subscription in November drew the attention of Dr. J. Livingston Thompson, one of the most eminent physicians of Indianapolis, who subscribed a hundred dollars, and in the letter accompanying his subscription offered, if occasion required, to be one of fifty persons to subscribe $500 each. Following Dr. Thompson's appeal came a letter from Lieut. Frank Eldridge, then of the United States cruiser " Chicago," commending the subscription and saying among other things : " If a beautiful silver service is placed in the wardroom of the INDIANA it will speak to foreigners in eloquent words of the character of Indiana, of its love of her and of its generosity."

Shortly after this W. W. Parsons, President of the Indiana State Normal School at Terre Haute, forwarded a subscription which had been taken up in the school. By cable there came from Peter Lieber, U. S. Consul at Düsseldorf, one hundred dollars. Francis Silas Cha'ard, Catholic Bishop of the Diocese of Vincennes, subscribed fifty dollars. The Hon. C. F. S. Neal, of Lebanon, Ind., at that time visiting in Montgomery, Ala., where he saw the great enthusiasm of that city in contributing for a gift to the cruiser "Montgomery," subscribed twenty-five dollars. On his return, Mr. Neal was influential in enlisting the attention of the Knights of Pythias, among whom he held high office, with the result as appears in the subscription list of many contributions by various lodges and by prominent members of the society. To his zeal, also, is due in part the splendid showing which the town of Lebanon makes in the same list.

The Terre Haute *Gazette*, the Franklin *News*, the New Albany *Public Press*, in these days contained urgent appeals for the work which had come to be looked on as a matter of State pride and patriotism. About this time the suggestion was made by Mr. Hendricks, School Superintendent of Jackson county, that collections be taken in the public schools. Although the suggestion was not generally adopted, Mr. Hendricks took up such a collection in Jackson county.

By this time the people, in voluntary associations, began to be heard from. The movement in the Knights of Pythias was begun by Arion Lodge. Washington Camp No. 5, Sons of America, also sent in a contribution, and George H. Thomas Post, G. A. R., of Indianapolis, contributed, being the first of the G. A. R. posts to do so. About this time the first offering from school children came in—the sum of fifty-three cents from the pupils of the Fountaintown school. The "Boys' Helping Club," in Indianapolis, contributed a dollar. The late Governor of Indiana and Minister to Mexico, Isaac P. Gray, sent in a contribution, and the Hon. Clem Studebaker, of South

Bend, for his manufacturing company, ended the year, December, 1894, with a hundred dollars, the sum subscribed during this year having amounted to nearly $1,800.

Lieut. David I. McCormick, of the Brigade Staff, Inspector of Small Arms, Indiana National Guard, who was greatly interested in the movement, started an appeal to the militia of the State. By letter aud circular and by personal effort, he got under way the movement resulting in so large a portion of the Indiana militia appearing in the subscription.

Sums from organizations of various kinds, militia companies, public schools and G. A. R. posts, were added in the early days of 1895. J. N. Marsh, the editor of the *Daily Times*, at Columbus, Ind., and Dr. Heckard, a dentist in the same town, took great interest in the contribution. Besides his own subscription, the latter gentleman endeavored, with some success, to interest the dentists of the State in this behalf. Mr. Marsh "enlisted for the campaign," and first and last was instrumental in forwarding the work appreciably.

The State Contributes to the Fund

During the early months of 1895, the Legislature of Indiana being in session, it was suggested by Robert Stockwell Hatcher, of Lafayette, then Reading Clerk of the Senate, and by others, that the sum of $2,000, remaining unexpended, of the appropriation made by the Legislature for the expenses of the State at the Columbian Exposition, be turned over to the battleship fund. Accordingly, on March 15, 1895, a concurrent resolution was adopted by the House and the Senate as follows:

"*Be it further resolved*, That the Board of Managers of said Columbian Exposition are hereby directed, immediately upon the passage of these resolutions, to pay to the Treasurer of State, out of any moneys in their hands, the sum of $2,000, taking his receipt therefor, which shall also be filed with the Auditor of State, and that the Treasurer of State shall pay said sum of $2,000 to Charles R. Williams, editor of *The Indianapolis News*, for the purchase of the silver service and library for the battleship INDIANA, whenever that sum will be sufficient, with the amount otherwise collected by said Williams, to complete the purchase-price thereof of $8,000."

The Halfway Point is Reached

The general subscription at this time amounted, in round numbers, to $2,000. By the action of the Legislature it was raised to $4,000. This appropriation is noteworthy as adding to the representative character of the subscription—a character which this subscription bears to an unusual degree.

At the halfway stage of the work one-half of the sum already raised is by individual contributions and by contributions from clubs, societies of various kinds, militia companies and schools; the other half is appropriated by the State, so that the people are represented in their political capacity as a

State as well as in their capacity as citizens and in their association in private societies.

Adding force and variety to the latter came immediately the movement of the Indianapolis Board of Trade, which subscribed $100 on its own account, and authorized its President to appoint committees to secure the co-operation of the boards of trade of Indiana, and to provide for canvassing the city of Indianapolis. It is to be noted at this point that thus far no such canvass had been made anywhere in Indiana. There had been no systematic solicitation of any kind. The growth of the subscription had been due entirely to the appeals in *The News* (written, nearly all, it should be said, by Mr. Morris Ross, the managing editor), to the words of other papers of the State and to the efforts of individuals, the chief of which have been mentioned, that were inspired by these appeals.

The School Children and the Fund

Late in March a very noteworthy addition was made to the fund; this was the balance remaining of the "penny fund" raised by the school children of the State for the educational exhibit at the Columbian Exposition. The suggestion that the balance be transferred to the fund was first made some months before by Mr. R. D. Smith, and this was promptly seconded by others. In December the County Superintendents' Association had taken action, as the following communication, addressed to the officers of the Board of World's Fair Managers, shows:

"Hon. Claude Matthews, Governor; Prof. John L. Campbell, President of the Board of World's Fair Managers; Hon. Fred J. Hayden, Treasurer of the Board of World's Fair Managers:

"GENTLEMEN—At a meeting of the County Superintendents' Association, held at the State-house, in Indianapolis, December 27, 1894, the following preamble and resolutions were offered and unanimously adopted:

"WHEREAS, The World's Fair Managers of Indiana gave their sanction to a plan and authorized the County Superintendents and teachers of the State to collect from the school children and school officials a 'penny fund,' with which to aid Indiana in making a 'school exhibit' at the World's Columbian Exposition; and,

"WHEREAS, There now remains in the hands of the Treasurer an unexpended balance of $463.37 of said fund,

"*Resolved*, That it is the sense of this association that the said balance should be applied to the battleship fund now being raised for the purpose of equipping the battleship INDIANA with a silver set.

"*Resolved*, That copies of these resolutions be furnished the Governor and the President and Treasurer of the World's Fair Managers, that they may act accordingly.

[Signed]   "F. M. SEARLES,
"Secretary County Superintendents' Association."

In March this matter was taken up by the Board of Managers, and the President and the Treasurer were authorized to turn the money over to the fund. The President's letter transmitting the warrant was as follows:

" INDIANAPOLIS, IND., March 29, 1895.

"*Mr. Charles R. Williams, Editor Indianapolis News:*

" DEAR SIR—I take pleasure in transmitting to you a warrant upon the Treasurer of the Board of World's Fair Managers for Indiana, Hon. F. J. Hayden, for the sum of four hundred and sixty-three dollars and thirty-seven cents ($463.37), as a contribution from the school children of Indiana to the fund for the purchase of a suitable silver service for the United States battleship INDIANA.

" This sum is the unused remainder of the 'penny fund' which was collected by the Committee on Education from the school children of the State for the use of the Educational Department of Indiana at the Columbian Exposition, and forms no part of the State appropriations.

" The Committee on Education, with the approval of the Executive Committee, has authorized me to make this disposition of the unused remainder of the fund at its disposal with the following conditions imposed:

" First—That a proper recognition of the donation as coming from the school children of the State shall be made in the selection and marking of a portion of the service.

"Second—That the selection and marking shall be subject to the approval of Hon. Claude Matthews, Governor of Indiana.

"Third—That the money hereby contributed shall be returned to Hon. F. J. Hayden, Treasurer, if the said silver service is not purchased.

"Very respectfully,

"J. L. CAMPBELL,

"President of the Board of World's Fair Managers for Indiana."

Thus all the school children of the State have a part in the service, and the most beautiful piece is inscribed as their gift.

Benjamin Harrison Contributes and Commends

On May 14, ex-President Harrison added a hundred dollars to the sum with the following letter:

"INDIANAPOLIS, IND., May 14, 1895.

"To the Editor of The Indianapolis News:

"I inclose you my check, to the order of Mr. Richards, for $100, to be added to the fund being raised for the purchase of a silver service for the battleship INDIANA.

"I hope the amount yet necessary will be speedily contributed by our citizens.

"The ship is a noble one; no better fighting ship is afloat; and our people should show their interest in her, and their appreciation of the fact that she bears the name of our State.

"Very truly yours,

"BENJAMIN HARRISON."

The Fund is Increased from Many Sources

May 21, Mr. John H. Holliday, President of the Union Trust Company, forwarded a hundred dollars, as subscribed by the Board of Directors of his company, this amount turning the $5,000 mark. The Grand Lodge of the State, Knights of Pythias, soon after subscribed a hundred dollars. Mr. Leroy J. Patty, of Carmel, Ind., a prominent member of this society, at the same time turned over to the fund thirty-five dollars due him from the Grand Lodge for special services.

There remained now $2,500 to be raised. Major C. T. Doxey, of Anderson, one of the best known men of Indiana, sent $125, saying he should like to do a little bit better than the largest individual subscription, which, to that time, was a hundred dollars. On the heels of this pleasant announcement, Dr. J. Livingston Thompson promptly subscribed fifty dollars more, making his sum $150, with the expressed wish that somebody would do better.

In these days—the early summer of 1895—small subscriptions were continually coming in, one of the many editorials in *The News* at this time, reading thus:

"We have the pleasure of again recording the enterprise of the Knights of Pythias in behalf of State pride and patriotism. Silliman Lodge, No. 66, of Rockville, and Greensburg Lodge, No. 148, each forwards a subscription. To have churches, schools, societies and fraternities, boards of trade, G. A. R. posts, militia companies and all the numberless combinations in which men find themselves represented in a response of this kind, is to increase its significance greatly."

This enumeration is typical of the sources from which contributions continued to come in. But belonging rather to the kind of effort exemplified by Major Doxey and Dr. Thompson, there came at this time an additional sum from Peter Lieber, at Düsseldorf, of ten dollars, which he desired to add to his first contribution of one hundred dollars. Late in July, 1895, just thirteen months after the beginning of the movement, *The News* contained an editorial of which extracts follow :

"There are two communications in this paper (among many others) to which we call especial attention. One is from the Brotherhood of Painters and Decorators, Union No. 47, located in this city. It forwards as this union's contribution to the battleship fund a check for ten dollars. The union uses a happy phrase. It asks the contribution to be 'placed to the credit of the Painters' Union No. 47, of Indianapolis.' There is a large truth in that. It is indeed to the credit of this union. It will be greatly to its credit. It speaks not for the amount, but for many times the amount in the patriotic impulse, the State pride and the determination which these workingmen show in their organized capacity to be represented among the citizens of Indiana in a gracious gift of this kind. The old phrase can be most truly applied to this case—it is not the gift but the giving. But better than the sum, far better, is the spirit that is back of it. The fine impulse that moves these men, without any solicitation, to take cognizance of this thing and to come forward as one of the patrons and creators of this contribution is noteworthy as well as significant.

"It is our good fortune also to call especial attention to the other communication, which is from the Secretary of the Business Men's Association of Evansville. It conveys one hundred dollars to the battleship fund. But in addition to this, Evansville has contributed two hundred and fifty-four dollars, making a total of three hundred and fifty-four dollars, and it accompanied its contribution with the cash. It was only Monday that, in speaking to this subject, we said that we ought, perhaps, to have two hundred dollars from Lafayette and twice that from Evansville. Within twenty-four hours Evansville had paid in three hundred and fifty-four dollars, and, it might be said, without any great concerted effort, and at a time when many of the most generous givers of the town were away. Another notable feature of the Evansville contribution is, that in the solicitation not one refusal was met with."

The Cities of the State are heard from

In August of this year there came through the instrumentality of Prof. Howard Sandison, of Terre Haute, a collection taken up at the Teachers' Institute of Daviess county. Through Mr. Sandison's initiative, several Teachers' Institutes in the State have part in this subscription, adding another phase to its wonderfully representative character.

Meanwhile Col. Wm. R. Holloway (Secretary of the committee, as afterward appointed by the Governor), visited several of the towns in the State, organizing and bringing to a focus the sentiment which had already found various expressions, with the result as noted in the subscription under the names of different towns. This stage of the work is reflected in the following extract from an editorial in *The News*, September 25, 1895:

"We print elsewhere a communication from Muncie, which forwards $243.50 for the fund for the Battleship INDIANA. This has been exceeded by only three cities—Evansville, which raised $357; and Terre Haute and Ft. Wayne, each of which raised $268. Logansport raised $197; Anderson, $187; Richmond, $73.50; South Bend, $96.12; Lafayette, $77; Kokomo, $53.50, and La Porte, $28.90. Assuming that the Indianapolis subscription will complete the $8,000, there has been raised in bits from $150 down to five cents, in round numbers, more than $5,500. The State contributes $2,000, and the 'penny fund' of the World's Fair, $463.67, making a total of $2,463.67 contributed independently of individual resource."

The Indianapolis Board of Trade Completes the Fund

There had gone forward meanwhile, under the auspices of the Indianapolis Board of Trade, through the committee it had appointed, a collection in the city of Indianapolis, which amounted to more than a thousand dollars, as the following letter shows:

"INDIANAPOLIS, October 7, 1895.

"*To the Governing Committee of the Indianapolis Board of Trade:*

"GENTLEMEN—Your committee, appointed to devise means of raising the remainder required with which to purchase a silver service and library for the battleship INDIANA, would respectfully report that sub-committees were appointed, and with their help the sum of one thousand one and 30-100 dollars ($1,001.30), exclusive of the one hundred dollars ($100) subscribed by the Board of Trade, was raised. Including this amount your committee is now prepared to turn over to the proper parties the sum of eleven hundred one and 30-100 dollars ($1,101.30), which we are happy to state completes the fund, and will enable the citizens of Indiana to present to the battleship named in honor of our State a silver service and library worthy of the great Hoosier State, and thus testify their appreciation of the honor that has been conferred upon them.

"Respectfully submitted,

"WILLIAM SCOTT, Chairman.
"FERD L. MAYER,
"C. C. PERRY,
"C. E. COFFIN,
"A. A. BARNES,
"F. A. MAUS,
"GEORGE R. SULLIVAN,
"*Committee.*"

The Committee was assisted in its work by other members of the Board of Trade as follows: D. M. Parry, J. J. Ryan, John R. Pearson, J. R. Henry, G. A. Schnull, W. H. Armstrong, H. W. Lawrence, Jacob W. Smith, John Wocher, F. E. Janes, H. E. Kinney, J. C. Walk, J. E. Bodine, T. J. Cullen and Hugh S. Byrkit.

The Board of Trade's collection raised the total of the popular subscriptions (with the "penny fund" balance) to more than six thousand dollars. Thus, with the amount appropriated by the Legislature now available, the fund proposed at the outset had been raised, and more too. Further effort to secure subscriptions was thereupon discontinued, but contributions still came in from time to time, as notably in October a subscription of one hundred dollars by cable from the directors of the Indianapolis Brewing Company, meeting in London. The money was rapidly collected, hardly a subscriber failing to respond. As soon as the money actually collected amounted to six thousand dollars, Auditor Daily and State Treasurer Scholz were called upon, and the Columbian Fair balance was paid over to the fund. This turned out to be not quite the two thousand dollars specified in the concurrent resolution, but it amounted to one thousand eight hundred and fourteen dollars and twenty cents ($1,814.20).

The Committee is Formed

The money was in hand. The part undertaken by *The News* was completed. The subscribers themselves were now called upon to finish the work. They were asked to meet at the Governor's parlors in the State-house, on October 15, to take the necessary action. A large number came together at the appointed time. Governor Matthews was made Chairman and Col. Wm. R. Holloway, Secretary. Charles R. Williams, editor of *The News*, reported briefly that the subscription was completed, and the money in bank ready to be turned over to the committee as soon as it should be appointed. He suggested that the meeting decide on the size of the committee and leave the appointment to the Governor, and at the request of the meeting he embodied his suggestion in a motion that the Governor be authorized to appoint a grand committee of twenty-five subscribers, of which he should be, *ex officio*, chairman, such committee to have the power to appoint sub-committees and to enlarge its number if it were found desirable; and to be intrusted with the expenditure of the fund, the selection of the design and all matters pertaining thereto. The motion was unanimously adopted, Governor Matthews announced that he would appoint the committee at a later date, and the meeting adjourned.

With the publication of the complete subscription list, which was made by *The News* four days later, on October 19, 1895, not quite sixteen months from the time it began the subscription, *The News* in an editorial recited the general character of the work, as has been fully set out above, concluding as follows:

" The list, which is, after all, not a long one, will well repay careful scrutiny. In addition to its representing the people and the school children of the State in the two sums mentioned, it represents individuals from every part of the

State, from some of the best-known citizens to children who contributed a few pennies. It represents the officials of the State from the Governor to mayors and subordinate officers. In all of the complex organization of modern life, it would seem that few of the associations in which men are gathered are unrepresented here. Moreover, except as already noted, the fund has come without personal solicitation or appeal, but as the voluntary and spontaneous gift of citizens, individually, and in their many associations, as already outlined. There was nowhere any importunity ; no fairs and solicitations of similar kind, which have been considered almost an inevitable concomitant of a great subscription, were needed in this case. The sums flowed from the enthusiasm, enterprise, pride and patriotism of the people of Indiana. Nothing more creditable than this to the good name of the State has been done.

"The greatest ship of our new navy, and believed to be the most powerful ship of its kind in the world, bears the name of our State. Following a gracious custom, Indiana has honored her namesake in keeping ; as it is the greatest ship, so Indiana has raised the greatest subscription, for it passes by some thousand dollars the subscription raised by the Empire State for the cruiser "New York," and no subscription, we are sure, has been more representative than this, and none so entirely expressive of the voluntary sentiment and free impulse of the people. It is a great work, greatly done. The people of Indiana have justified the confidence which *The News* expressed in their temper, their kindliness and their pride. They have honored themselves.

"This enterprise has now reached the place where this paper lays down its work. Our work as a distinct part ceases and is merged in the whole. We have been the means of enabling the people of Indiana to do an act, and to do it well, that reflects increasing honor on our goodly State. We undertook it simply as one influence in the life of the people. A thing of this kind was everybody's business, and, therefore, likely to become nobody's business. It was necessary, if it was to be done, and done as it should be done, that some one should make it his business. *The News* made it its business. It became the means and medium of calling the attention of the people to it, and this, as we said at first and have never ceased to say, was all that was necessary to do the work. Our faith has been confirmed by the work. All honor to the people of Indiana."

October 22, Governor Matthews announced the names of the committee, as follows:

Governor Claude Matthews, Chairman *ex officio*.

Ex-President Benjamin Harrison.

General Lew Wallace, Crawfordsville.

Judge John H. Baker, Goshen.

Francis Silas Chatard, Bishop of the Diocese of Vincennes.

Mayor Thomas Taggart.

Ex-Mayor Caleb S. Denny.

I. S. Gordon, President of the Indianapolis Board of Trade.

William Scott, Chairman of the Board of Trade INDIANA Committee.

General W. J. McKee, Commander First Indiana Brigade.

Dr. J. Livingston Thompson, Indianapolis.

John H. Holliday, Indianapolis.

John P. Frenzel, Indianapolis.

L. S. Ayres, Indianapolis.

William R. Holloway, Indianapolis.

Charles R. Williams, Indianapolis.

T. S. Blish, Seymour.

Hon. Clem Studebaker, South Bend.

Hon. C. F. S. Neal, Lebanon.

Hon. S. P. Sheerin, Logansport.

Hon. W. R. McKeen, Terre Haute.

Hon. C. T. Doxey, Anderson.

Hon. J. H. Bass, Ft. Wayne.

Hon. John J. Nolan, Evansville.

Hon. Arthur W. Brady, Muncie.

Hon. James S. Reynolds, Lafayette.

Executive Committee Named and Work Begun

The grand committee met at the State-house, October 25, nearly all of the members being present, and completed its organization by electing John H. Holliday Treasurer, and William R. Holloway Secretary.

A general discussion then ensued with relation to the best disposition of the fund. It was decided that the proposed library should be limited to a selection of books by representative Indiana authors and of books relating to Indiana. This decision was determined by the fact that the Government places an admirable general library on every man-of-war. Thus the greatest part of the fund would be left for the proposed silver service, which the committee desired should be conspicuous by reason of artistic workmanship, and should, in its ornamentation, have features distinctively representative of the State. To carry out the details of the work in hand it was decided that it would be well to create an executive committee. This committee was to consist of the three officers of the grand committee and six others to be appointed by the chairman. A few days later Governor Matthews announced this committee, as follows:

> Governor Claude Matthews, Chairman.
> John H. Holliday, Treasurer.
> Col. Wm. R. Holloway, Secretary.
> Gen. Lew Wallace.
> Dr. J. Livingston Thompson.
> Hon. Thomas Taggart.
> Hon. S. P. Sheerin.
> Hon. Arthur W. Brady.
> Charles R. Williams.

The Executive Committee met November 15, and completed its organization by choosing Charles R. Williams as Vice-

Chairman. The first matter to be decided was the general character of the proposed silver service, the number of pieces and their purpose, and then to agree on a plan of securing designs and estimates from the leading silversmiths of the country. Information was laid before the committee in regard to services presented to other naval ships, together with suggestions from Admiral Brown of the Navy.

After prolonged discussion the committee directed that the vice-chairman should visit Philadelphia, Baltimore and New York to consult with the chief silversmiths of those cities in regard to the number and character of the pieces that should constitute the proposed service, and also to get such other information as would be useful to the committee.

Designs and Bids Invited

The visit was made early in December. After hearing Mr. Williams's report, the chairman was instructed to address a letter to the principal silversmiths of the country specifying the pieces desired, and inviting them to submit under cipher designs and bids. The letter concluded with these words:

"The committee has few specific suggestions to make as to the character of the designs. In general, it may say that it has no craving for bigness or gorgeousness or overornamentation. It does not believe that anchors and ropes and other hackneyed and commonplace motives of decoration are absolutely essential. What it seeks is graceful outlines, with a dignified and thoroughly artistic scheme of decoration. Each piece should somewhere bear a reproduction of our State seal, as the State has no coat of arms. And if practicable, as the committee believes it will be, the Indiana State Soldiers' and Sailors' Monument should be drawn upon for decorative motives. The State is famous for its hardwood forests—black walnut, oak, maple, sycamore, beech, etc.; corn and wheat flourish as in few other States; the wild rose, golden rod and asters brighten every field and wayside. Perhaps in some of them are decorative motives."

Designs Accepted and Contract Let

The designs and bids were to be submitted by February 1. Six houses entered the competition: The Gorham Co., The Whiting Co., Dominick & Haff, and Tiffany & Co., all of New York; The Bailey, Banks & Biddle Co., of Philadelphia, and Samuel Kirk & Son, of Baltimore. The Executive Committee met at the Governor's parlors February 5, and spent nearly the whole day in the careful examination of the designs. Three sets of designs were agreed upon as superior to the others, and of these one was unanimously selected as preferable, if slight changes could be secured. When the ciphers were opened it was found that the winning designs were those of Tiffany & Co., and the other two sets the work respectively of Dominick & Haff and Samuel Kirk & Son. The Executive Committee thereupon adopted the following resolution:

"*Resolved*, That Vice-Chairman Charles R. Williams be requested to visit New York, to confer with Tiffany & Co., and request that they make such modifications in their proposition to furnish a silver service for the battleship INDIANA, as to the number of pieces, designs, weights and price as the said Williams may suggest, and should the said Tiffany & Co. agree to said changes, Charles R. Williams is hereby authorized to sign a contract on behalf of this committee with said Tiffany & Co., for the manufacture of a set of silver service."

Mr. Williams visited New York within the next few days and found Tiffany & Co. willing to make all the modifications which had seemed desirable to the committee. Thereupon the contract was completed and the work on the service was immediately begun. The service was finished in July; it was exhibited by Tiffany & Co. for a few days at their store in Union Square, where it attracted great attention and praise; it was then exhibited early in August in Indianapolis, under the supervision of Julius Walk & Son, at the store of Albert Gall, where it was admired by all that saw it.

The Presentation of the Service

The presentation of the service and the library was made on board the INDIANA in New York bay, off Tompkinsville, September 21, 1896. A party of Indianians composed of men belonging to the grand committee or to the Governor's staff, with members of their families or guests, went on to New York to be present on that occasion. In the party were: Governor

Matthews, Mrs. Matthews, Miss Matthews and Miss McMechen; Bishop F. S. Chatard; Mayor Thomas Taggart, Mrs. Taggart and Miss Lucy Taggart; Mr. C. S. Denny and Mrs. Denny; Mr. I. S. Gordon; Brigadier-General W. J. McKee and Mrs. McKee; Dr. J. Livingston Thompson and daughter, Mrs. Oliver; John H. Holliday and son, Alexander Holliday; William R. Holloway; Charles R. Williams, Miss Lucy L. Williams and Mrs. Morris Ross,—all of Indianapolis; the Hon. Clem Studebaker, South Bend; Major C. T. Doxey, Mrs. Doxey and Mrs. Kinnard, of Anderson; the Hon. S. P. Sheerin and Mrs. Sheerin, of Logansport; Mr. T. S. Blish, of Seymour; Adjutant-General Irvin Robbins and Mrs. Robbins, Colonel William Foor and Mrs. Foor, Surgeon-General R. French Stone, Colonel James B. Curtis, Lieutenant-Colonel John H. Murphy, Mrs. Murphy and Miss Florence Coffin, Colonel James R. Ross and Mrs. Ross, all of Indianapolis; and Majors A. B. Mewhinney and George W. Gagg, of Terre Haute. There joined the party at New York, Ex-President Harrison and Mrs. Harrison; Rear-Admiral George Brown, Mrs. Brown and George Brown, Jr.; Lieutenant-Colonel Thomas Defrees and several Indiana people resident at New York or who happened to be there.

The Navy department detailed the dispatch boat " Dolphin " to take the party to the INDIANA. The " Dolphin " was boarded shortly after ten o'clock off the West Thirty-fourth street dock, Mr. Harrison being welcomed with a salute of twenty-one guns. Captain Clover and Assistant-Secretary McAdoo did the honors. The "Dolphin" steamed down the bay and passed between the ships of the White Squadron which lay at anchor in two lines off Tompkinsville. There were the "New York," the flagship of the squadron, which fired a salute of seventeen guns in honor of the assistant-secretary, the "Maine," "Indiana," "Columbia," "Raleigh," "Montgomery" and "Massachusetts." On all, the officers and men were drawn up in line and the bands played as the "Dolphin" went by. The "Dolphin" passed on through the Narrows into the lower bay to give the landsmen a real taste of salt air, and not far from Sandy Hook dropped anchor, when a delicious luncheon was served. After that the "Dolphin" turned about and came back to the INDIANA, her arrival being welcomed by a general salute of seventeen guns from all the ships of the squadron. General and Mrs. Harrison, Governor Matthews and family and Admiral Brown and wife were first transferred to the INDIANA, where they were received by Captain Evans, Lieutenant-Commander Swift and other officers. The other members of the party were rapidly transferred. On board the INDIANA were Rear-Admiral Bunce and nearly all the officers of the squadron. The marines were in line and all the men of the crew were massed on the after-deck. There the silver service was seen, displayed upon the stars and stripes. About this the whole company gathered when Governor Matthews stepped forward and made the presentation speech.

Governor Matthews's Speech

"*Captain Evans*—We are here to-day representing the citizens of a great inland State, to greet you on the sea, and to express, in part, a grateful recognition of an honor conferred upon the State, which justly holds our loyal devotion. Indiana felt truly honored when this magnificent vessel and powerful engine of war was christened with her name, and yet with pardonable pride we, citizens of Indiana, feel that she could wear upon her massive sides or float from her masthead no prouder name.   [Cheers.]

"A great ship, a triumph of the ingenuity of man, should well be coupled with a great State, whose greatness rests upon the generous gifts of God, and their wise development and ennobling use by man.

"To you, sir, as commander, we bring this tribute of our people, so truly expressive of their culture, their generosity and their patriotism, and we beg you to accept it for the good ship INDIANA, for the use of yourself, your officers and those who may worthily come after you, to walk these decks beneath the flag of the free American citizen, whether upon the land or upon the sea.

"For this gift was prompted and encouraged by the highest sense of patriotism, contributed as it was by toilers on the farm and in the workshop, by men in the professions, by citizens of every vocation, high and low, rich and poor, and last, but not least, by the children of our schools, where early are taught the lessons of a sublime devotion to country, a supreme reverence for its laws and its flag.

"It may be appropriate to speak a brief word on this occasion to you—whose great misfortune it is not to have been a child of Indiana, and which you doubtless appreciate,—about the great State we 'hail from,' and in the achievements of which our hearts are filled with just and pardonable pride. Indiana, in the central part of that vast domain we call our common country, and to-day the center of population, is, through soil and climate and position in the highway of progress, best located for the highest physical and intellectual development. The pioneers, a sturdy, manly race of farmers, who first pierced the dense umbrageous forests of Indiana, braving the dangers of a new and unknown country, and facing merciless foes, came with stout hearts and strong arms, the advance guard in the grand march of civilization, to lay the foundation of an empire, and rear their children in a noble, self-reliant manhood. What a pathetic sublimity in the record of their humble lives! And could we but read in full the simple annals of the earnest struggle, the daily sufferings and sacrifice, what a glory would encircle the memory of the men and women of that day! [Cheers.]

"Indiana, entering the sisterhood of States but eighty years ago, is small in area as compared with many others; but God has been so bountiful in his blessings bestowed, her soil is so rich, that she has long been placed in the front rank of agricultural and grain-producing States through the energy, the industry and the enterprise of her sons. In other resources, how rich and wonderful—with the finest quality of coal underlying over six thousand square miles of her territory; the unexcelled building stone, evidenced in many splendid buildings in this great metropolis; the as yet unknown supply of gas and oil, underlying nearly one-half her area! With great manufactories and thriving cities springing up everywhere; with beautiful lakes and rivers, and over 7,000 miles of railroad, and all these intelligently developed by a wise, cultured, industrious and progressive people—who could undertake to paint the picture of Indiana's future? With even step have her people kept pace with this material development in the wisdom and humanity of her laws and government. In no State and among no people have been laid the foundations of a broader or more generous educational system, which has been copied in a great degree by every State following Indiana into the Union of States.

"There is, too, a broad humanity in the care of the unfortunate and afflicted, and her ample and hospitable institutions eloquently speak of the charity and justice of her people. I will not weary you with a review of the achievements of Indiana's sons and daughters in all the fields of literature, science and art. And that Indiana does not forget services rendered in time of peril is manifested in a beautiful monument, the grandest in our country, erected by her grateful citizens to the memory of the soldier and the sailor who risked all in defense of their country.

"When the danger thickened, and the life of the Government, as founded by our fathers, was in doubt, the sons of no State responded more promptly to the call of their country, and their blood stained the battlefields from Philippi to the firing of the last gun, away down on the Rio Grande.

"The name given to this great battleship has been made an honored one by a brave, generous and intelligent people. If true to this name, we shall have no fear for the future of the battleship INDIANA—beautiful and majestic in peace, terrible in war, bravely defending and jealously guarding the safety, the honor and the dignity of our country. [Cheers.]

"Before closing, it is just and proper that he, who was the inspiration of the sentiment which is now fulfilled to-day in the presentation of this silver service, should have that credit due—Mr. Charles R. Williams, of *The Indianapolis News*. He gave unsparingly and untiringly of his time and labor. We all in the name of the State rejoice in the success which has crowned his earnest efforts.

"In conclusion, no small gratification comes to us that this presentation may be made at a time when a son of Indiana, Rear-Admiral Brown, whom we rejoice to have with us to-day, is the ranking officer of this navy, and at a time when this ship is in command of one who has at all times and on all occasions shown a courageous devotion to his country and a lofty fidelity to duty. I beg you, Captain Evans, in behalf of the people of Indiana, to accept this silver service as an expression of the appreciation of the honor bestowed upon their State." [Cheers.]

Charles R. Williams's Speech

At the conclusion of his speech, Governor Matthews called upon Mr. Charles R. Williams, who spoke as follows :

"*Captain Evans, Ladies and Gentlemen*—The very kindly reference of Governor Matthews to my part in the affair which here to-day reaches its happy culmination is at once very embarrassing and very pleasing to me. My part throughout has been one of delightful experiences and of deepening consciousness of the intensity of American patriotism. I have looked forward to this day with glad anticipation. It is one of the happiest incidents in a busy and laborious career.

"Let me say, however, that my part, or rather our part, to use the editorial plural, which indeed is the appropriate form in this connection—our part, the part played by the paper I edit, was only that of a voice giving articulate expression to the pride and the appreciation of a great people that so staunch a warship should bear the name of the State they honor and love. The voice spoke, the people responded, the good work was done. Without the spirit to appeal to, the voice had been a voice crying in the wilderness. The credit is not to the voice, except in that it recognized opportunity as obligation, but to the people whose spirit gave it glad accord.

"Indiana is not a mere geographic appellation. It is a history, where devoted missionaries follow her water-courses to plant the cross among the savage tribes; where George Rogers Clark and his little army penetrate the pathless wilderness and do heroic deeds ; where men from the southland fix their homes that they, for conscience sake, may free their slaves; where men of Puritan strain from New England and men of Cavalier descent from Virginia clasp hands to found a commonwealth and mingle their blood to make a race strong, sturdy and resourceful. It is a sentiment. To the sons and daughters of that fair State, the very mention of the word brings a thrill of patriotic pride. It is steeped for them in all the tender associations of home, in the consciousness of all the achievements of a worthy past, in the prophecies and potencies of a splendid future. It brings to them a sense of the heroism of the war period when every seventh person in the State bore arms in the strife for union and freedom. It recalls the names of the great men that have illustrated the annals of the State—Clark and Wayne and William Henry Harrison, Morton and Gresham, Hendricks and McDonald, Wallace and Riley, and first and last—soldier, orator, statesman, citizen—Benjamin Harrison. [Cheers.]

" Governor Matthews has dwelt with special emphasis on the wonderful material wealth and prosperity of the State. And this is well, for they bespeak the industry and thrift of our people. And these things too are the necessary condition precedent in preparing the soil for the finer flowering of the things of the spirit. And herein Indiana is no mean State. In the things that speak of the higher life she has much to her credit. Art and architecture, music and social culture, science and learning, literature and oratory, are sincerely cultivated and esteemed as in few parts of the land. The great story of Ben Hur circles the world with its throng of readers; the poems of Riley sing themselves into the hearts of all that speak the English tongue.

"To us of Indiana the name this great ship bears means all this and more. And so out of our love for the name sprang our pride and joy that it should be bestowed on the first great battleship of the new navy. It is a worthy name. May the ship bear it worthily! Out of our pride and joy sprang the desire to signify our appreciation of the honor to the State in some way that should be manifest to all that may be of this ship. It is not the gift, therefore, but the giving that means most. It is not the thing itself, though it be a thing of beauty and so will be a joy forever, but the thought that lies behind the thing, that is significant. Our gift is an outward and visible sign of an inward and spiritual grace of patriotism and State pride.

"'Peace hath her victories
No less renowned than war.'

"The Government, mindful of the wise saying of Washington, 'to be prepared for war is one of the most effectual means of preserving peace,' has built the great warships not that war may come but that peace may be insured. It has mightily equipped the INDIANA that if there should be need to strike she may strike hard for victory. We of the far inland, where no shock of naval warfare can ever be heard, equip you with this superb artillery for peaceful conquests. We are sure that when you direct this upon your guests they will at once capitulate, and that you and they, for the time being at least, will have no division of sentiment on the silver question. [Laughter and Cheers.]

" So through the future, wherever this ship may ride at anchor, while the glorious flag at the topmast speaks of the common country and the name upon the prow recalls how the Union is strong because of the strength and character of the units that compose it ; while her massive sides of steel proclaim her power of passive resistance, and these terrible deep-throated guns breathe of aggressive might ; this silver service, with its artistic loveliness of form and its suggestive symbolism of ornamentation, and these books that throb with life in all its more gracious uses, that sing of quiet peace and happy homes, shall bring to mind that the system of government, under which life may be so free to develop and so beautiful in its development, is a system worth building and maintaining such great and powerful ships as this to defend and to fight for. While the spirit of patriotism which built this ship and which inspired this gift survives we can be confident our ship of state will sail all seas in safety.   Ship and gift are material and artistic embodiment of the prayer and faith of Longfellow :

> " ' Thou, too, sail on, O Ship of State,
> Sail on, O Union, strong and great,
> Humanity with all its fears,
> With all its hopes of future years,
> Is hanging breathless on thy fate !
> In spite of rock and tempest's roar,
> In spite of false lights on the shore,
> Sail on, nor fear to breast the sea !
> Our hearts, our hopes, are all with thee,
> Our hearts, our hopes, our prayers, our tears,
> Our faith triumphant o'er our fears,
> Are all with thee,—are all with thee ! ' "
> [Cheers.]

Assistant=Secretary McAdoo's Speech

The gift was received on behalf of the officers of the INDIANA by William McAdoo, Assistant Secretary of the Navy, who spoke as follows :

" I esteem it a very great honor to be allowed to speak for the officers and men of the INDIANA in the receipt of this splendid present. Here we have a delegation of leading citizens of one of the great States of the Union, occupying an imperial position in the central West, and far removed from the seaboard, headed by their Governor, present here to-day on board of this mighty engine of national power to testify to their pride and interest in this ship, the name she bears and the flag she carries. The spectacle illustrates that this ship belongs in common to the people of a great country having a most extensive territory, in which, however, no part is alien to the other, and every American is brother to the other, and we are all children of our common mother, the indestructible and ever united republic. The people of Indiana demonstrate that they admire this ship and love the flag she carries no less and no more than those of us who live here on the seaboard, and that they and we are the citizens of a common country, united in a common interest, devoted to a common glory, jealous to the same degree of our national honor and interests, devoted to the same principles and animated by the same lofty feelings of nationality.

" The name of this ship, the first modern battleship of

the United States, was very happily chosen after a State situated geographically in the very heart of our territory, a splendidly typical American commonwealth, rich in the history of heroic deeds and great names, and bearing witness to an exalted patriotism, whether on the field of battle or in the no less momentous conflicts for the honor and welfare of the nation in times of peace.

"The custom of naming these ships after States and communities was for a long time one about which men differed. Many were in favor of preserving those pleasant sounding and thoroughly American Indian names which formerly studded the Naval Register, and others thought that we should have made the ships monuments to our national heroes by giving to them their names; but on the whole I think a very wise course was pursued when it was determined that these names should be those largely of States and communities, thus fostering a personal and local pride in our new navy. There is a great deal in a name, because even in the most practical of ages sentiment continues and will continue to be a most potent factor in all human affairs. There is not a coward on board of this ship, and I am sure there never will be one, but if she went into battle and there was one son of Indiana on board of her I am sure that if he got an opportunity the inspiration of her name would make a hero of him, and in such a conflict I know that each of you would feel a dear and tender personal interest in every man on board. The naming of these battleships, too, after States is a very happy illustration of the basic principles of our Republic. This ship at once testifies to two apparently irreconcilable forces, local sovereignty and national power—forces happily blended and indestructibly fused in our country. The great State of Indiana proudly gives her name to this fine ship which represents the imperial strength of the Republic on its outer borders and says to her: 'Defend well the shore and we will by our civic virtues, and if need be by our valor, preserve intact the honor and glory of our country on the land. We are proud of our State but prouder of our country.' [Cheers.]

"Speaking for the officers and men of the INDIANA, I can assure you that they very heartily and earnestly appreciate this princely present, and that they will exhibit it in every port where they may go, at home or abroad, not only for its beauty and intrinsic value, but as an unanswerable demonstration of the unity of our people, the intensity of their national feeling, and the just pride which they have in the navy of the United States ; exhibiting through it to the world the loving fraternity and unsectional devotion which permeate the domain of the Republic and make our people, whether in the center or on the sea, one in hearty desire and honest aims for the best interests of the country, the preservation of its honor, the maintenance of its dignity and the assertion of its rights.

"The ship is worthy of you and your State. If she has any equal of her tonnage either in offensive or defensive qualities it is not known to the naval experts. She is truly a

magnificent monument to the inventive genius, the earnest
endeavor, the industry and skill of our people. She represents the
whole sum of human knowledge of the mechanic and scientific
arts. To produce this great floating fortress great secrets have
been wrested from nature and every art of man has attained
its highest degree. Her enormous battery, beyond all precedent in naval architecture, may well be taken as a fit illustration of the concentrated energies of our people, their quick
action and invincible determination. It has been said in some
quarters that we are not the originators of this type of ship,
and that we have copied European models. This statement is
more superficial than real. We are the originators of all the
battleships of Europe. The "Monitor" was the idea from
whence sprung the whole of modern navies. Recuperating for
twenty-five years from the effects of a tremendous civil war,
the other nations pushed out invention to its fullest limit, but
within a short period of twelve years we entered boldly into
competition with the acquired experience of twenty-five, its
wealth and machinery, and, without boasting, we to-day cer-
tainly can challenge comparison with the work done in any
part of Europe, and in this very ship we have made bold if not
startling and successful innovations upon all battleships here-
tofore built. Well may you be proud of her, as the officers and
men are proud of you and of your gift. You need have no fears
for her safety in peace or in war under any circumstances or
in any peril, but that from her brave and battle-scarred captain
to the youngest apprentice boy on board she will carry your flag

in the path of honor and glory, and will never suffer it to go down until the last life has been sacrificed under its folds. It is your flag, it is our flag, it is sacred in all parts of our land, as sacred as the cross of Christ to the Christian, and we shall live to keep it free and honored, and die, if necessary, to see that it is never lowered to any foe at home or abroad."

[Prolonged cheers.]

Ex-President Harrison's Speech

When the cheers ceased, in response to a general call Mr. Harrison stepped forward. He was greeted with enthusiastic and prolonged cheers. He spoke impromptu but in his happiest vein, saying, in substance:

" I am delighted to be here and to witness this magnificent spectacle. I am especially delighted because of the fact that I am a sort of grandfather to this ship. I confess the fact the more willingly because she is so young a ship. When I was in a position to have some influence with the Secretary of the Navy, I told him I wanted the best ship then building to be named after Indiana, and I think he followed out my wish. [Cheers.]

"A company of Indiana people have come here to-day— just those that could get away—to express their pride in this ship, their love of the flag and their confidence in the men the INDIANA carries. This magnificent silver service pleases silver men and gold advocates alike. Governor Matthews takes pleasure in the sheen of the white metal, while Mr. Williams rejoices in the fact that so much silver will never reach the mint. Here is free silver, Captain Evans, and in all that this means is Indiana a free-silver State. [Cheers and laughter.]

"We have wrought wonders in the building of our navy. When I was a senator I recall with much regret the partisan jealousy manifested in reconstructing and rebuilding the navy. It mortified me then, and I rejoice now that we have passed that state of affairs, and that congress does not pause now to consider whether we have a Democratic or a Republican Secretary, when asked to build additions to our navy, out of fear of filling up the navy yards for election purposes. The progress made in our navy has been amazing. The countries of Europe had spent millions of dollars upon their navies, while we fell behind for twenty-five years after our civil war. Now we come in to reap all the benefits of the blunders and outlay of those countries. We have marched up to them, until we now stand abreast of the greatest naval constructions of the world. Who says we shall not go beyond them?

"There are navies in the Old World greater than ours, and there probably always will be. England has set herself the enormous task of keeping her naval strength as great as that of any three European powers combined. She needs such a navy because her army is small, and because she must look out for her numerous colonies and her great commercial interests in all parts of the globe.

"We do not need so large a navy, but we do need a powerful navy. We are a commercial people, and our commerce is extending. Our people are scattered all over the earth. We send missionaries to far-off lands. We must take care of them. We must have ships to speak of our power at home, and when necessary the commanders must clear their decks for action to protect our citizens from outrages.

"Our foreign policy has been a sentimental one; our sympathies have gone out to every suffering people fighting for freedom. But we are not going to seize other people's territory; we are not a nation of filibusters. But other nations are doing so; the world is not big enough for them. They are, on one pretense or another, appropriating the territories of the weak powers and tribes. But there is a hemisphere here in which we have an interest. We can not consent that it shall be sliced up and divided among the great European powers as Africa has been. Our people are holding congresses of arbitration. This is all very well, but have you not noticed that demands for fixed sums as indemnity for supposed injuries are never made upon a country that has battleships like this? How these ships do enforce a diplomatic note! We must get out into the seas everywhere and look after our citizens, and protect and extend our commerce."

Mr. Harrison then proposed "three cheers for the good ship, the officers and men, and the flag above her," and the cheers were heartily given.

Then Captain Evans stepped forward, saying: "My lads, three cheers for the men who gave us this silver," and the INDIANA resounded with the lusty shouts of the gallant crew.

The guests were then taken on a tour of inspection over the ship, after which they were transported to the "Dolphin," which conveyed them back to New York.

Letter of Gift

In making the presentation Governor Matthews handed to Captain Evans a formal letter of gift, a copy of which follows:

"INDIANAPOLIS, Sept. 21, 1896.

"*Captain Robley D. Evans, Commanding U. S. Battleship Indiana:*

"DEAR SIR—In the name of the committee selected to represent the subscribers to the purchase fund, I have the honor herewith formally to present through you to the battleship INDIANA the silver service and the collection of books by Indiana authors which are now placed in your possession.

"The silver service is a gift to the ship for the use of all the commissioned officers who shall serve in her, and it is the desire of the committee that when any mess of commissioned officers of the INDIANA shall give an entertainment it shall be entitled to use all or any part of the service for such occasion.

"I have the honor to be

"Very truly yours,

"CLAUDE MATTHEWS,

"*Chairman of the Battleship Fund Committee.*"

Description of the Service

The silver service consists of a full dinner service and a tea set. Altogether there are thirty-eight pieces, most of them large and massive. The keynote of the artistic and graceful decorations is the beautiful centerpiece. It is a large flower or fruit dish of elaborate workmanship and delicate finish. The hand of the designer makes it appear lighter in weight than it really is. It is ten inches high and twenty-eight inches long. Its weight is 297 ounces, nearly twenty-five pounds. The shape is oblong, with delicately curved handles at each end. In the center, on each side, is a medallion; on one the seal of the State of Indiana is borne in high relief, while on the other, also in high relief, is a *fac-simile* in miniature of the Soldiers' and Sailors' Monument at Indianapolis. Similar medallions appear on all the pieces. Curving outward from these medallions are shells of the nautilus entwined with seaweed in varied forms, and pendant from these are wreaths of eglantines, oak and sycamore leaves, shrubs, etc., symbolizing the flora of the State. Underneath the medallion is an inscription: "From the School Children of Indiana," this being the piece to which the "penny fund" was devoted. The graceful rolling form suggests the rolling swell of the sea, while the under-curve recalls the lines of a clipper ship. The piece is richly gold-lined, and over the top is a silver-gilt wire-network covering for cut flowers, which can be removed, when the dish can be used as a jardiniere; or if the lining is taken out, it will also serve as a fruit-dish.

Ranking next to this in richness of effect come the massive candelabra; these have nine lights each, and stand twenty-two and a half inches high, exclusive of candles and shades, and weigh over thirty-six pounds. The arms of the candelabra are gracefully twined, and the sconce cups and saucers are formed of the eglantine flowers. The large salver, another notable piece, is oblong in form, twenty-four inches long, and weighs over two hundred ounces. The salver has two handles, and in the large open center space there is a fine etching, measuring eleven inches, of the Soldiers' and Sailors' Monument. Beneath the monument, in the center of an elaborate bit of ornamentation, appears the seal of the State of Indiana, and also the words: "Presented to the Battleship INDIANA, by the Citizens of Indiana, 1896." A similar inscription has been introduced as a decoration upon the punch-bowl. In addition to these inscriptions, there is etched upon the underside of each piece:

BATTLESHIP INDIANA

PART OF SILVER SERVICE PRESENTED

BY THE CITIZENS OF INDIANA

The handsome tea-set, consisting of tea-kettle, stand and lamp, tea-pot, coffee-pot, sugar-bowl, cream-pitcher and slop-bowl, weighs over two hundred ounces, so that the tray and tea service alone weigh over thirty-four pounds. Then there is the massive punch-bowl, with a capacity of four gallons. In this piece to the general decorations have been added grape leaves and large bunches of the fruit. The bowl stands eleven inches high, measures nineteen and one-half inches in extreme width at the top, and weighs about eighteen pounds.

The remaining pieces consist of a twenty-four-inch meat-dish, intended for a large roast; a twenty-six-inch fish-dish, an eighteen-inch meat-dish; two round thirteen-inch entrée dishes; two gravy-boats; two double vegetable-dishes, arranged so that by unlocking the handles from the top, the covers are converted into dishes; four compotiers, all lined with gold, standing six and one-fourth inches high; two large fruit-dishes; one very handsome ice-cream dish, with richly decorated lattice work drainer; one ice-cream slicer; one salad-bowl, spoon and fork, all lined with gold; one ice-bowl and tongs, four hors d'œuvre dishes, gold-lined; and one water-pitcher with a capacity of ten pints.

The service was designed by Mr. John T. Curran, of Tiffany & Company's silver factory, and in its entirety contains nearly two hundred pounds of sterling silver $\frac{925}{1000}$ fine.

The silver is fitted into three handsome and substantial oak chests, lined with red chamois and bound with brass, and bearing brass plates suitably inscribed.

List of Books

Morton, O. P.—Memorial Addresses on the Life and Character of O. P. Morton.
Morton, Oliver T. The Southern Empire.
McCulloch, Oscar C.—The Open Door.
McCulloch, Hugh—Men and Measures of Half a Century.
Nicholson, Meredith.—Short Flights.
Nowland, J. H. B.—Reminiscences of Early Indianapolis.
Nowland, J. H. B.—Sketches of Prominent Citizens.
Parker, Benjamin S.—Cabin in the Clearing.
Parker, Benjamin S.—Hoosier Bards.
Riley, James Whitcomb.—Pipes o' Pan.
Riley, James Whitcomb.—Afterwhiles.
Riley, James Whitcomb.—Rhymes of Childhood.
Riley, James Whitcomb.—Flying Islands.
Riley, James Whitcomb.—Neghborly Poems.
Riley, James Whitcomb.—Green Fields.
Riley, James Whitcomb.—Sketches in Prose.
Riley, James Whitcomb.—Armazindy.
Riley, James Whitcomb.—Poems Here at Home.
Riley, James Whitcomb.—Old Fashioned Roses.
Smith, Oliver H.—Early Indiana Trials and Sketches.
Smith, William Henry.—The St. Clair Papers. Two volumes.
Stein, J. A.—History of the Army of the Potomac.
Sulgrove, Berry.—History of Indianapolis and Marion County
Terrell, W. H.—Indiana in the War of the Rebellion.
Thompson, Maurice.—The Witchery of Archery.
Thompson, Maurice.—The King of Honey Island.
Thompson, Maurice.—Poems.
Thompson, Maurice.—A Tallahassee Girl.
Thompson, Maurice.—Lincoln's Grave.
Thompson, Richard W.—Papacy and the Civil Power.
Thompson, Richard W.—Recollections of Sixteen Presidents. Two volumes.
Thompson, Richard W.—Footprints of the Jesuits.
Stephenson, David.—Indiana Roll of Honor.
Walker, Chas. M.—Sketch of the Life, Character and Services of O. P. Morton
Wallace, Lew. Ben Hur.
Wallace, Lew. Prince of India.
Wallace, Lew. The Fair God.
Wallace, Lew. The Boyhood of Christ.
Wallace, Mrs. Susan E. The Storied Sea.
Wallace, Mrs. Susan E.—Land of the Pueblos.
Wallace, Mrs. Susan E.—Repose in Egypt.
Woollen, William W.—Biographical and Historical Sketches of Early Indiana.
Wylie, Theophilus A. A History of Indiana University.

List of Subscribers

STATE CONTRIBUTIONS

THE STATE OF INDIANA, by concurrent resolution of the two Houses of the General Assembly, transferring to the fund the balance of the Columbian Fair appropriation.

THE SCHOOL CHILDREN OF THE STATE, by action of the trustees of the "penny fund," contributed to aid the Indiana Educational Exhibit at the Columbian Fair, transferring th balance of the said fund to the battle-ship fund.

POPULAR CONTRIBUTIONS

Federal and State Officers

Benjamin Harrison, Ex-President of the United States.

Claude Matthews, Governor of Indiana.

Albert G. Porter, Ex-Governor Indiana and Ex-United States Minister to Italy.

John W. Foster, Ex Secretary of State of the United States.

General Lew Wallace, Ex-United States Minister to Turkey.

John H. Baker, Judge United States District Court.

David Turpie, United States Senator.

Isaac Pusey Gray, Ex-Governor, and United States Minister to Mexico.

Alonzo Greene Smith, Attorney-General of Indiana.

J. O. Henderson, Ex-Auditor of Indiana.

William R. Myers, Ex-Secretary of State of Indiana.

Albert Gall, Treasurer of Indiana.

A. M. Sweeney, Clerk Indiana Supreme Court.

Timothy E. Howard, Judge Indiana Supreme Court.

Americus C. Daily, Auditor of Indiana.

Wm. D. Owen, Secretary of State of Indiana.

George G. Tanner, Surveyor of the Port of Indianapolis.

Albert G. Sahm, Postmaster of Indianapolis.

Peter Lieber, United States Consul at Düsseldorf, Germany.

Oliver T. Morton, Clerk United States Court, Chicago.

Members Indiana Legislature

Justus C. Adams, Indianapolis, Speaker of the House.
W. H. Leedy, Indianapolis.
John McGregor, Indianapolis.
W. C. Van Arsdel, Indianapolis.
Charles F. Remy, Columbus.
James W. Hamrick, Danville.
H. M. McCaskey, Point Isabel.
F. E. Holloway, Evansville.
Albert Kamp, Evansville.
W. E. Blakely, Shelbyville.

City and County Officers, Indianapolis

Caleb S. Denny, Mayor.
J. E. Scott, City Attorney.
P. C. Trusler, City Comptroller.
Sterling R. Holt, Treasurer Marion County.
Thomas Taggart, Auditor Marion County and Mayor Indianapolis
Frank McCray, Judge Criminal Court.
J. W. Fesler, County Clerk.
Albert A. Womack, Sheriff.
W. B. Holton, President Board of Works.
John Osterman, Board of Works.
E. L. Atkinson, Board of Works.
Dr. Franklin W. Hays, President Board of Health.
E. F. Claypool, President Park Board.
F. A. Maus, Park Board.
Lee Nixon, City Clerk.
Col. W. R. Holloway, Mayor's Clerk.
Charles C. Brown, City Engineer.
Bart Parker, Clerk Board of Works.

The Indiana Militia

Staff Officers First Brigade, Brigadier General W. J. McKee, Commanding.
Officers Second Indiana Regiment.
Company C, First Regiment, New Albany.
Company G, First Regiment, Jeffersonville.
Company I, First Regiment, Greencastle.
Company K, First Regiment, Princeton.
Company B, Second Regiment, Rochester.
Company C, Second Regiment, Anderson.
Company D, Second Regiment, Indianapolis.
Company G, Second Regiment, Covington.
Company K, Second Regiment, Clayton.
Indianapolis Companies, Second Regiment, Collection at Annual Church
Service.
Company F, Third Regiment, South Bend.
Company K, Third Regiment, Auburn.
Company M, Third Regiment, Indianapolis.
Battery C, First Artillery, Rockville.

Organized Bodies

GRAND ARMY OF THE REPUBLIC

I. N. Walker, Commander-in-Chief, G. A. R.
George H. Thomas Post, Indianapolis.
Dupont Post, Shelbyville.
Houghton Post, Mishawaka.
Baldwin Post, Vernon.
Rich Mountain Post, Lebanon.
George H. Chapman Post, Indianapolis.
Paton Post, La Porte.
Auten Post, South Bend.

KNIGHTS OF PYTHIAS

Grand Lodge, Indianapolis.
Arion Lodge, No. 254, Haughville.
Pythagoras Lodge, No. 380, Indianapolis.
Scipio Lodge, No. 363, Scipio.
Star Lodge, No. 7, Indianapolis.
Dana Lodge, No. 247, Dana.
Venus Lodge, No. 43, Jamestown.
Shield Lodge, No. 71, Frankfort.
Lebanon Lodge, No. 45, Lebanon.
Ladoga Lodge, No. 54, Ladoga.
Thorntown Lodge, No. 124, Thorntown.
Silliman Lodge, No. 66, Rockville.
Greensburg Lodge, No. 148, Greensburg.
Palestine Lodge, No. 137, Bedford.
Alexandria Lodge, No. 335, Alexandria.
Ascalon Lodge, No. 155, Princeton.
Damascus Lodge, No. 384, Indianapolis.
Robert Owen Lodge, No. 72, New Harmony.
Booneville Lodge, No. 64, Booneville.
Sicilian Lodge, No. 234, Pendleton.
La Grange Lodge, No. 144, La Grange.
Fortville Lodge, No. 404, Fortville.
La Porte Lodge, No. 112, La Porte.
Oriental Lodge, No. 81, Terre Haute.
Winamac Lodge, No. 274, Winamac.
Greenwood Lodge, No. 278, Greenwood.
Iola Lodge, No. 53, Richmond.

TEACHERS' INSTITUTES

Daviess County Institute, by Howard Sandison.
Johnson County Institute, by Howard Sandison.
Fountain County Institute.
Miami County Institute.
Franklin County Institute.
Spencer County Institute.
Gibson County Institute, by F. D. Churchill.
Marion County Institute.

PUBLIC SCHOOLS

State Normal School, Terre Haute, by Pres. W. W. Parsons.
Fountaintown Public School.
Irvington Public School.
Johnson County Schools, through E. L. Hendricks, Superintendent.
Knightstown Public School.
La Porte Public School.
High School, Lebanon.
District No. 11, Pike Township, Marion County.
Colored School No. 2, Shelbyville.
South Bend Schools.

VARIOUS ORDERS AND SOCIETIES

Loyal Legion, Indiana Encampment.
Loyal Legion, Richmond.
Woman's Relief Corps, Worthington.
Hiawatha Tribe, No. 75, Improved Order of Red Men, Indianapolis.
Red Cloud Tribe, No. 18, Improved Order of Red Men, Indianapolis.
Patriotic Sons of America, Washington Camp, No. 5, Indianapolis.
Patriotic Sons of America, Washington Camp, No. 3, Rushville.
Patriotic Sons of America, Washington Camp, No. 6, Crawfordsville.
Patriarchs Militant, No. 42, I. O. O. F., Indianapolis.
Ancient Order Hibernians, Indianapolis.
Sons of American Revolution, Anthony Wayne Chapter, No. 1, Fort Wayne.
Washtella Council, No. 37, D. of P., Muncie.
Young Men's Institute, Indianapolis, through J. D. Brosnan, Treasurer.
Painters and Decorators' Union, No. 47, Indianapolis.
Gospel Temperance Union, Indianapolis.
Boys' Helping Club, Indianapolis.
Literary Society, New Augusta.
Young People's Society Christian Endeavor, Christian Church, Greenfield,
    proceeds of entertainment.

Corporations, Indianapolis

Indianapolis Board of Trade.
The Union Trust Company.
Pettis Dry Goods Company.
The Indianapolis Water Company.

The Indianapolis Brewing Company.

Builders' Exchange.

Indianapolis Chain and Stamping Company.

Indianapolis Harness Company.

Indiana Bicycle Company.

Comstock & Coonse Company, Pump Manufacturers.

Kingan & Company, Limited, Pork Packers.

The Gordon-Kurtz Company, Harness, etc.

The Hide, Leather and Belting Company.

The Home Stove Company.

The Indianapolis Light and Power Company.

The Indianapolis Gas Company.

The Model Clothing Company.

The Evans Linseed Oil Company.

The Rockwood Manufacturing Company, Founders.

The Pioneer Brass Works.

The Clabourne Burner Company.

The Grocers' Manufacturing Company.

The Sinker-Davis Company, Machinists.

The State Bank of Indiana.

The People's Outfitting Company, Furniture, etc.

The Bowen-Merrill Company, Publishers and Booksellers.

The Indiana Cigar Company.

The Central Rubber and Supply Company.

Arthur Jordan Company, Butter, Eggs and Poultry.

Krug-Reynolds Company, Wholesale Grocers.

Indiana Paper Company.

Indianapolis Drug Company.

Climax Baking Powder Company.

Indiana Lumber and Veneer Company.

Laycock Manufacturing Company and employes, Spring Beds, etc.

The Avery Planter Company.

The Indianapolis Plumbing Company.

The Indianapolis Paint and Color Company.

The May Mantel and Tile Company.

A. Burdsall Company, Paint Manufacturers.

Firms, Indianapolis

The Indianapolis News.
Julius C. Walk & Son, Jewelers.
E. C. Atkins & Company, Saw Manufacturers.
Taylor & Smith, Leather and Belting.
Hayes & Ready, Wholesale Liquors.
Pearson & Wetzel, Wholesale Queensware.
James R. Ross & Company, Wholesale Liquors.
Murphy, Hibben & Company, Wholesale Dry Goods.
W. J. Holliday & Company, Wholesale Hardware.
Severin, Ostermeyer & Company, Wholesale Grocers.
Francke & Schindler, Wholesale Hardware.
Baldwin, Miller & Company, Wholesale Jewelers.
Freaney Brothers, Plumbers.
Knight & Jillson, Steam, Water and Gas Supplies.
Kruse & Dewenter, Furnace Manufacturers.
Schrader Brothers, Wholesale Grocers.
J. N. Millikan & Company, Contractors and Builders.
Bliss & Swain, Clothing.
S. H. Knox & Company, Notions.
Gordon & Harmon, Agricultural Implements.
Charles Mayer & Company, Toys, Fancy Goods and Notions.
L. S. Ayres & Company, Dry Goods.
R. S. McKee & Son, Wholesale Boots and Shoes.
D. P. Erwin & Company, Wholesale Dry Goods.
McKee & Company, Wholesale Boots and Shoes.
Fahnley & McCrea, Wholesale Millinery.
Kothe, Wells & Bauer, Wholesale Grocers.
Griffith Brothers, Wholesale Millinery.
Daggett & Company, Wholesale Confectionery.
Ward Brothers, Wholesale Druggists.
Young & McMurray, Merchant Tailors.
E. L. Leonard & Company, Men's Furnishing Goods.
Bockhoff Brothers, National Cash Register.
Brosnan Brothers, Dry Goods.
T. M. Hervey & Company, Ticket Brokers.
Hawkins & Shaw, Proprietors Sherman House.

Stubbins & Watson. Proprietors Stubbins Hotel.

The Armstrong Laundry.

Doherty & Burns, Cigars.

Collier & Murphy, Funeral Directors.

Healy & O'Brien, Plumbers.

Blum & Company, Grocers.

M. S. Huey & Company, Planing Mill.

Adams & Williamson, Veneer Manufacturers.

Dedert & Sudbrock, Dry Goods.

W. P. Scott & Company, Carpenters and Builders.

George Merritt & Company, Woolen Manufacturers.

Reid Bros, Real Estate.

Bertermann Brothers, Florists.

Boicourt, Tyner & Company, Monuments.

Hotze & Wilde, Bicycles.

Montani Brothers, Orchestra.

"Pap's" Stores, Dry Goods.

E. S. Rich & Son.

Individual Subscribers, Indianapolis

Dr. J. Livingston Thompson.

John H. Holliday, Banker.

John P. Frenzel, Banker.

Otto N. Frenzel, Banker.

Volney T. Malott, Banker.

Albert J. Beveridge, Lawyer.

Leon Bailey. Lawyer.

John L. Griffiths, Lawyer.

Alfred F. Potts, Lawyer.

Augustus Lynch Mason, Lawyer.

Albert Baker, Lawyer.

I. N. Harlan, Lawyer.

J. F. Carson. Lawyer.

Howard Cale, Lawyer.

Charles E. Coffin, Real Estate.

Francis Silas Chatard, Catholic Bishop Diocese of Vincennes.

D. B. Knickerbacker, Protestant Episcopal Bishop Diocese of Indiana.

Rev. D. O'Donaghue, Rector St. Patricks.

John S. Spann, Real Estate.

Miss Jessie Miller (who christened the INDIANA).

Miss Alice Newell.

Miss Mary A. Williams.

Charles T. Whitsett, Funeral Director.

Clemens Vonnegut, Jr., Merchant.

J. H. Claypool, Lawyer.

Wm. L. O'Connor, Merchant.

Charles R. Williams, Editor *The Indianapolis News.*

J. M. Tilford, Retired Business Man.

Morris Ross, Managing Editor *The Indianapolis News.*

Dr. T. C. Faries, Dentist.

E. H. Eldridge, Lumber Dealer.

D. M. Parry, President Parry Manufacturing Company.

V. K. Hendricks, Wholesale Boots and Shoes.

Charles Letler, Wholesale Hats.

Newton Todd, Loans and Insurance.

Henry Sweetland, Expressman.

George Sadlier, Horseshoer.

Joseph Haas, Medicines.

O. A. Robertson, Wholesale Confectioner.

J. H. Dilks, Manager Indianapolis Natural Gas Company.

H. Ringolsky, Queensware.

C. Krauss, Driven Wells.

George Cook, Livery.

John Rauch, Cigar Manufacturer.

T. A. Conlee, Agricultural Implements.

J. W. Smith, Secretary Board of Trade.

Louis Siersdorfer, Retail Shoe Dealer.

William B. Burford, Printer.

Edward Hawkins, Manager Indiana School Book Company.

George W. Hayler, Passenger Agent C., H. & D. Railroad.

George W. Sloan, Druggist.

William T. Marvy, Jeweler.

Fred Brandt, Restaurant.

F. H. Ruppert, Furniture and Stoves.

W. L. Resoner, Furniture.

George R. Sullivan, Wholesale Tinners' Supplies.

G. A. Schnull, Wholesale Groceries.

William Scott, Wholesale Drugs.

W. A. Applegate, Sugar and Tea Broker.

Frank S. Fishback, Coffee Broker.

C. E. Kershner, Restaurant.

William H. Armstrong, Surgical Supplies.

H. W. Lawrence, Proprietor Spencer House.

J. A. Wenell, Hatter.

A. Quigley, Milliner.

B. Samuels, Milliner.

C. W. Kriel, Newsdealer.

H. Cohen, Pawnbroker.

Joseph Solomon, Pawnbroker.

Frank M. Ryan, Hatter.

J. Ungericht, Barber.

F. T. McQuiddy, Men's Furnishings.

H. F. Ganon, Cigars.

W. H. Smith, Engraver.

Emil Willbrandt, with W. H. Armstrong & Company.

J. H. Wells, Barber.

J. D. Adams, Sewer Pipe and Bridges.

R. Ryse, Township Trustees' Supplies.

S. M. Hice, Merchant Policeman.

N. J. McConney, Cigars.

J. W. Bryan, Drugs.

Harry A. Moran, Saloon.

M. Selig, Dry Goods.

George W. Koehne, Proprietor Normandie Hotel.

J. A. Papadopulos, Fruit Dealer.

D. W. Engle, Saloon.

John Stroble, Bartender.

John S. Sebern, Cigars.

W. N. Short, Drugs.

J. G. Hollenbeck, Passenger Agent I., D. & W.

George K. Powell, Saloon.

J. B. Harter, Saloon.

C. P. Webb, Ticket Broker.

George Hotz, Merchant Tailor.

George W. Frey, Ticket Broker.

N. E. Lenaghan, Saloon.

C. Van Camp, Wholesale Hardware.

D. H. Jenkins. Publisher *Jersey Bulletin.*

Charles G. Grah, Razor Grinder.

E. E. Matthews, Printer.

T. Kearney, Druggist.

John Agnew, Saloon.

M. M. McElwaine, Gas and Water Supplies.

N. H. Kipp, Agent Empire Fast Freight.

L. V. Boyle, Lumber.

L. L. Fellows, Agent Midland Fast Freight Line.

W. M. Gerard, Ticket Broker.

F. R. Taylor, Bookkeeper.

Daniel Stewart, Wholesale Drugs.

Julius D. Pearson, Druggist.

M. O'Connor, Wholesale Grocer.

Louis H. Levey, Printer.

A. A. Barnes, Woodenware Manufacturer.

Leopold Leppert, Merchant Tailor.

Henry W. Langenberg, Saloon.

John B. Siessl, Saloon.

M. Woolf, Saloon.

Thomas F. Powers, Saloon.

H. A. Wise, Restaurant.

H. C. Schergens, Jeweler.

Frank Gisler, Saloon.

F. W. Mucho, Cigars.

A. Steffen, Cigars.

Louis Feller, Jeweler.

Joseph C. Pfleger, Sewing Machines.

Henry G. Reger, Cigars.

Frank E. Brown, Boots and Shoes.

W. H. Ballard, Creamery.

Frank E. Janes, Flour and Feed.

D. Eagan, Horseshoer.

P. J. Flanedy, Newspaper Solicitor.

H. Haynes, Restaurant.

M. H. Daniels, Justice of the Peace.

John Freiburg, Harness and Saddlery.

Samuel V. Perrott, Real Estate.

Henry Meyer, Real Estate.

John Wocher, Insurance and Real Estate.

E. Y. Gaston, Grocer.

Fred Kolb, Saloon.

R. F. Catterson, Real Estate.

George N. Catterson, Real Estate.

W. S. McMillen, Agricultural Implements.

H. A. Davis, Tinner.

Joseph Gardner, Tinner.

Joseph K. Sharpe, Jr., Secretary Indiana Manufacturing Company.

Dennis O'Brien, Saloon.

H. M. Foltz, Cashier D. H. Baldwin & Company.

W. H Mansfield, Merchant Tailor.

R. E. Stephens, Sewing Machines.

E. Lung, Laundry.

William Ward, Picture Dealer.

Peter B. Kellenberger, Confectioner.

J. W. Gray, Upholsterer.

C. Hagedon, Harnessmaker.

C. W. Nickum, Baker.

W. F. Clemens, Bicycles.

F. L. Bryant, Jeweler.

J. E. Gorman, Laborer.

A. O. Dochez, Druggist.

C. D. Hoover, Bicycle Repairer.

Henry Smith, Saloon.

E. R. Scott, Baker.

John F. White, Agent Casualty Company.

M. T. Campbell, Jeweler.

Walter S. Pouder, Beekeepers' Supplies.
W. E. Templeton, Plumber.
Frank H. Carter, Druggist.
L. E. Haag, Druggist.
H. W. Krause, Men's Furnishings.
Otto Neerman, Shoemaker.
C. Neerman, Shoemaker.
John O. Cooper, President Industrial Life Association.
A. W. Williams, Carpet Weaver.
H. Latham, Interior Hardwood Company.

City Engineer's Office, Indianapolis

Geo. R. Boyce.	Edward Hill.
J. B. Cameron.	B. J. T. Jeup.
George Champe.	E. A. Kingsley.
Wm. W. Christ.	Louis Kline.
J. H. Dean.	F. P. A. Lingenfelter.
H. A. Dill.	W. S. Mellender.
A. O. Ewan.	S. H. Moore.
H. H. Fletcher.	John T. Owens.
Joseph Foppiana.	George W. Seibert.
F. E. Fuller.	Thomas Tallentire, Jr.
Harry Haymond.	Fred Yount.
Wm. H. Harrison.	

Marion County Sheriff's Office, Indianapolis

R. P. Craft.	R. E. Scott.
J. A. Dynes.	Addison Townsend.
Andrew Hogan.	G. Walter Charles.
Henry List.	Wm. W. Walden.

Marion County Clerk's Office, Indianapolis

John R. Clinton.	John A. Hugg.
J. F. Fesler.	

Letter Carriers, Indianapolis

John Amos.
A. H. Arbuckle.
James Barnhill.
Wm. E. Bassett.
Charles A. Boyle.
A. E. Bragdon.
J. C. Brown.
James Cantlon.
Ed. Carskadon.
J. P. Cochrane.
R. S. Cochrane.
R. S. Coxe.
E. W. Crane.
Isaac Doll.
C. F. Doran.
Joseph A. Downey.
E. R. Ellis.
Frank Faris.
J. H. Garver.
W. W. Hall.
M. W. Healey.
J. N. Hobbs.
Charles V. Hoover.
Wm. J. Hufford.
Wm. E. Jones.
Wm. Kirchmaier.
C. W. Kuetemeier.
B. J. Lantz.
W. N. Leonard.

Fred A. Lorenz.
Albert Magley.
J. Mathias.
R. L. Maze.
Frank Meredith.
Will S. Mitchell.
J. L. Moore.
R. H. McGinnis.
Alex. McNutt.
J. D. Porter.
Geo. W. Reed.
F. C. Rogers.
Gus. Schmedel.
R. O. Shimer.
Grant Smithson.
I. N. Smock.
Aaron Stern.
J. M. Stutsman.
Geo. W. Sulgrove.
A. A. Taylor.
J. M. Taylor.
James L. Tipton.
H. M. Trimpe.
John J. Turner.
R. W. Wadsworth.
Wm. S. Warner.
W. C. Weber.
A. J. Wells.
John Wren.

Unclassified

J. B. Plessinge.

S. B. Straus.

Children of Morton Place.

Master James B. Higgins.

Master Harry Blaine Dynes.

Willie Dickson.

M. B. Wilson.

Fred Perry.

C. Worrell.

Li Chung, Brookville.

E. E. Barbour.

H. Johnson.

F. Schrader.

T. J. Gerard.

W. O. Darnall.

John Faehr.

Many contributors in various places who did not give their names.

Anderson

Major C. T. Doxey, Capitalist and Manufacturer.

W. T. Durbin, Banker.

Dr. H. E. Jones, Physician.

Edmund Johnson, Clerk of Madison County.

M. D. Harmon, Recorder of Madison County.

Cambridge City

P. T. Hinkley.

Carmel

Leroy J. Patty.

Columbus

J. N. Marsh, Editor *Times*.

Dr. W. A. Heckard.

Dr. S. E. Whitesides.

Others through the *Times*.

Evansville

Hon. R. D. Richardson, Judge Circuit Court.
Kiechle, Brentano & Oberdorfer, Stove Foundry.
Rietman & Schulte, Saw Mill.
E. W. Matthews, Manager John Gilbert Dry Goods Co.
Blackman & Lunkenheimer, China and Glassware.
W. W. Ross, Assistant Editor *Journal-News*.
Business Men's Association, by W. W. Rosencranz, President.
Von Behren Manufacturing Co., Spokes, etc.
Orr, Griffith & Co., Iron, Steel, Wagon Wood Works.

Ragon Brothers, Grocers.
I. Gans, Notions.
Charles Leich & Co., Drugs.
Boetticher, Kellogg & Co., Hdw.
R. K. Dunkerson, Capitalist.
Vickery Bros., Grocers.
Parsons & Scoville, Grocers.
Samuel Bayard, Banker.
The John Ingle Coal Co.
The John Gilbert Dry Goods Co.
S. P. Gillett, Banker.
Bank of Commerce.
H. J. Schlaepfer, Druggist.
William E. French & Co, Carpets.
Holt & Brandon, Ice and Cold Stor.
Phœnix Flour Mill.
Evansville Ice and Cold Stor. Co.
Newton Kelsay, Manufacturer.
Blount Plow Works.
Evansville Woolen Mill Co.
Single Center Spring Co.

H. Wilkiemeyer, Supt. Gas Works.
John A. Reitz & Sons, Saw Mill.
Heilman Plow Co.
Heilman Machine Works.
John J. Nolan, Postmaster.
First National Bank.
M. J. Bray, Jr., Capitalist.
The F. W. Cook Brewing Co.
Evansville Brewing Association.
The Buehner Chair Co.
H. D. Moran, Supt. Street R'y Co.
The John G. Neumann Co., Com'n.
S. W. Douglas, Photographer.
C. F. Artes, Jeweler.
W. H. Keller. Printer.
A. Bitterman, Jeweler.
Smith & Butterfield, Book Store.
R. Haueisen, Toys and Notions.
P. Hermann, Manufacturer.
Meyerhoff & Kahn, Stove Foundry.
S., W. & C.

Ft. Wayne

Dr. Seneca B. Brown, Dentist.
The Isaac Knapp Dental Coterie.
Root & Co., Merchants.
Louis A. Centlivre, Brewer.
J. B. White, Grocer.
Samuel M. Foster, Manufacturer.
A. E. Hoffman, Lumber.
S. Bash & Co., Produce Merchants.
Chas. McCulloch, Banker.
H. C. Hanna, Lawyer.
O. S. Hanna, Bank Cashier.
O. P. Morgan, Hardware.
H. M. Williams, Capitalist.
J. H. Bass, Banker and Iron Founder.
E. H. McDonald, Wholesale Grocer.
G. E. Bursley & Co., Wholesale Grocers.

A. I. Friend, Clothier.
Pixley & Co., Clothiers.
W. W. Rockhill, Postmaster.
D. N. Foster, Furniture.
J. O. Bond, Bank Cashier.
C. W. Edsall, County Auditor.
A. D. Cressler, Iron Founder.
Wm. Geake, Contractor.
C. E. Bond, Bank Teller.
Gross & Pellens, Druggists.
Wm. H. Dreier, Druggist.
E. F. Clansmeier, Sheriff.

Greenwood

Whiteland Military Band and receipts from concert for benefit of fund.
John A. Polk, Farmer.
Dr. Z. Carnes.
Dr. Joe Wishard.
Hon. James E. Watson, Lawyer.
Rev. L. L. Turney.
Dr. G. C. Fisher.

Chas. F. Coffin, Attorney.
Geo. Robertson, Farmer.
James Neighbors.
W. H. Dunlavy, Sanitarium.
James Kelly, Farmer.

Kokomo

H. G. Woody, Superintendent of City Schools.
Armstrong, Landon & Hunt Co., Manufacturers.

R. Ruddell, Banker.

O. V. Darby, Merchant.

V. D. Ellis, Clerk Court.

T. S. Strickland, Merchant.

Drs. Ross and Cox.

Dr. J. B. Kirkpatrick.

W. F. Ruddell, Contractor.

J. F. Elliott, Attorney.

W. L. Benson & Co., Contractors.

M. Bell, Attorney.

Blacklidge & Shirley, Attorneys.

Chas. A. Styer, County Treasurer.

J. E. Moore, Attorney.

M. Garrigus, County Auditor.

J. M. Leach & Co., Manufacturers.

J. A. Kautz, Editor *Tribune*.

E. E. Springer, Real Estate.

H. E. Henderson, Editor *Dispatch*

G. O. Roach, Grocer.

D. E. Murphy, Real Estate.

W. C. Purdum, Attorney.

M. F. Brand, Real Estate.

O. A. Somers, Farmer.

A. A. Covalt, Manufacturer.

Lafayette

Hon. E. P. Hammond, ex-Judge Circuit Court.
Brown Brockenbrough, Bank Cashier.
H. W. Emerson, Printer and Stationer.

James M. Reynolds, Capitalist.

Wm. V. Stuart, Lawyer.

James M. Fowler, Banker.

W. M. Blackstock, Retired Farmer.

M. A. Kennedy, Postmaster.

The George A. Bohrer Brewing Co.

Wm. W. Smith, Banker.

P. A. Byers, Saloon.

Chas. S. Warner, Banker.

La Porte

The Wadsworth Co., Newspaper Publishers.

E. F. Michael Co., Manufacturers Fanning Mills.

Niles & Scott Co., Manufacturers Wood and Metal Wheels.

The Rumely Co., Mfrs. Separators.

La Porte Carriage Co., Manf'rs.

John W. Russert, Brewer.

King & Fildes Co., Woolen Mfrs.

Edward Molloy, Journalist.

F. W. Meissner, Jr., Druggist.

F. H. Doran, County Auditor.

O. A. Whitmer, Teacher.

J. R. Fraser, Grocer.

G. H. Carter, Painter.

J. W. Crumpacker, Banker.

W. D. Spore, Express Agent.

W. A. Banks, Farmer.

F. R. Carson, Mayor.

J. J. Stedman, Dentist.

W. F. Porter, Broker.

G. H. Hastings, Merchant.

Ben Kramer, Merchant.

Davidson & Porter, Merchants.

Dr. H. K. Ehrlich, Druggist.

J. Barnes & Co., Merchants.

S. E. Grover, Postmaster.

D. C. Peters, Druggist.

Dr. E. J. Church, Dentist.

Fredrickson & McLane, Merchants.

William Crawford, Merchant.

M. Kreidler, Jr., Merchant.

John Lonn, Merchant.

G. A. Talbert, Teacher.

D. Levinson, Merchant.

J. C. Scarce, Merchant.

S. Lay & Son, Merchants.

J. Q. Hamilton, Hotel Man.

Stebbins S. Webber, Merchant.

Dr. N. G. Dakin, Physician.

Lebanon

C. F. S. Neal, Real Estate.

George F. L. Essex, Bookkeeper.

Ben F. McKey, Editor.

Joe King, Barber.

Harry T. Thompson, Merchant.

Dr. W. H. Schultz, Physician.

John H. Perkins, Merchant.

James W. Batterton, Contractor.

John H. Halfman, Saloon.

Harry J. Martin, Editor.

George W. Campbell, Lumberman.

Emil Schoback, Tailor.

Joseph A. Coons, County Sup't.

Rev. J. A. Knowlton, Baptist Minister.

Sone of Veterans.

Thos. J. Powell, Retired Farmer.

Phil Adler, Merchant.

Lafayette Wilson, Merchant.

David W. Foster, Merchant.

Dr. A. P. Fitch, Physician.

Samuel R. Artman, Attorney.

Charles M. Zion, Attorney.

Shadrick Sanders, Laborer.

Guy A. Schultz.

Charles S. Riley, Retired Farmer.

Charles W. Scott, Clerk Circuit Ct.

David W. Osborn, County Treas.

Logansport

Hon. Daniel P. Baldwin, Attorney.

W. T. Wilson.

Nelson & Myers, Attorneys.

Hon. S. P. Sheerin, Capitalist.

John F. Johnson, Banker.

J. M. Bliss, County Clerk.

George B. Forgy, Broker.

William H. Brown, Retired.

A. J. Murdock, Banker.

Logansport and Wabash Valley Gas Co.

Louthain & Barnes, Publishers *Pharos*.

H. Wiler & Co., Carpets.

Elliott & Co., Wholesale Grocers.

W. H. Bringhurst, Drugs.

J. W. Henderson & Sons, Furniture.

C. B. Stevenson, Shoe Dealer.

J. C. Hadley, Furniture.

Logan Milling Co.

Andy Welsh, Grocer.

C. F. Rauch, Shoe Dealer.

S. T. McConnell, Attorney.

Madison

The Courier and many subscribers.

Muncie

Joseph A. Goddard, Wholesale Grocer.

John J. Hartley, Real Estate Dealer.

Henry L. Hopping, Prosecuting Attorney.

Arthur C. Pershing, Township Trustee.

Robert W. Monroe, County Auditor.

Capt. W. J. Hilligoss, Real Estate Dealer.

George F. McCulloch, President Street Railway Company.

Reuben Thompson, County Recorder.

James Boyce, Manufacturer.

Ed Tuhey, Postmaster.

George L. Lenon.

Arthur W. Brady, Attorney.

T. F. Rose, Attorney.

Thomas Morgan, Contractor.

Hardin Roads, Banker.

A. L. Johnson, Manufacturer.

Edward Olcott, Banker.

R. J. Beatty, Manufacturer.

Indiana Iron Co.

Ball Bros. Glass Man'f'ing Co.

J. C. Johnson, Banker.

D. A. Lambert, County Treas.

R. G. Hemingray, Manufacturer.

C. M. Turner, Banker.

John M. Kirby, Lumber Dealer.

W. E. Hitchcock, Banker.

Fred Klopfer, Carriage Maker.

J. H. Smith, Manufacturer.

F. B. Nickey, Druggist.

Frank T. Reed, Liveryman.

M. Cohen, Junk Dealer.

O. N. Cranor, Attorney.

John E. Reed, County Clerk.

T. H. Barton, City Treasurer.

W. A. Spurgeon, Physician.

New Albany

Hon. Charles L. Jewett.

New Castle

W. H. Elliott.

Plainfield

T. J. Carlton, Superintendent Reform School.

Princeton

Thomas R. Paxton.

Rensselaer

Erastus Peacock.

Richmond

Hon. William D. Foulke, Capitalist and Author.
Hon. Henry U. Johnson, Member Congress.
George H. Knollenberg, Merchant.
John M. Gaar, Manufacturer.
Joseph B. Craighead, Manuf'r.
Milton B. Craighead, Manuf'r.
George P. Early, Manufacturer.
W. G. Scott, Manufacturer.

John M. Lantz.
Wm. P. Cook.
George R. Williams.
Perry J. Freeman, Lawyer.
A. H. Bartel.

Scipio

A. B. Kieter.

Seymour

Mrs. Sarah S. Blish, The Blish Milling Co.

South Bend

Studebaker Brothers' Mfg. Co., Wagons, etc.
Hon. George Ford, Lawyer and ex-Congressman.
Edwin Nicar, Correspondent at Oliver Plow Works.
L. Pine, General Manager Singer Mfg. Co.
Christian Sieg, Mason and Contractor.

O'Brien Varnish Co. — No. 2 Hose Company.
George Watters Ford. — Fanny Potter, Student.
W. H. Oren, County Treasurer. — Hungarian Citizens.
George M. Fountain, County Clerk. — Harry D. Johnson, Jr., Student.
Robert Myler, ex-County Auditor. — South Bend Toy Mfg. Co. Empl'y's.
Eli Herring, Carpenter. — L. Eliel, Druggist.

Terre Haute

Spencer F. Ball, City Editor *Gazette.*
G. A. Conzman, Cashier Vigo County National Bank.
N. Filbeck, Proprietor New Filbeck Hotel.
Preston Hussey, President National State Bank.
Hon. G. W. Faris, Congressman Fifth District.
F. McKeen, Cashier McKeen & Co., Bankers.
Col. Daniel Fasig, Commission Merchant.

W. R. McKeen, Capitalist. — F. C. Goldsmith, Traveling Man
Hon. Fred A. Ross, Mayor. — Terre Haute Brewing Co.
George M. Allen, Editor *Express.* — H. Hulman, Wholesaler.
J. P. Suttie, Traveling Man. — Terre Haute Savings Bank.

West Newton

Wesley Allen. — Levi Paddock.

Report of the Treasurer

RECEIPTS.

Received account	popular subscription from The Indianapolis News ..		$5,374 33
"	"	Appropriation from State of Indiana..	1,814 20
"	"	"Penny Fund"	463 37
"	"	Subscription to Indianapolis Board of Trade	1,001 30
"	"	Interest on funds in hands of Treas...	237 76
		Total receipts	$8,800 96

DISBURSEMENTS.

Paid Tiffany & Co. for Silver Service	$7,785 00
" For Library	144 98
" Wm. R. Holloway, salary and expense while making collections through the State	266 85
" C. R. Williams, Vice-Chairman of Committee, expense of trips to Cincinnati, Baltimore and New York in December, 1895, to secure designs, etc.	63 45
" C. R. Williams, expense of trip to New York to complete contract	23 00
" Express charges on Silver Service to Indianapolis and return	60 90
" Exchange on New York draft (Tiffany & Co.)	7 78
" Stationery	10 00
" For Historical Publication	195 00
" For invitations to presentation	30 00
" For postage and telegrams	12 47
*Cash balance on hand	291 53
	$8,890 96

JOHN H. HOLLIDAY, Treasurer.

*The Executive Committee has ordered that this balance be used to purchase a permanent memorial of the INDIANA in the shape of a picture to be hung in the Governor's parlor at the State House.